Dot Markers Activity Book

Happy Halloween

With BIG DOT Circles

Ages 2+

This book is made to be used with paint daubers or dot markers. Each page has a black background on the reverse to help with bleed-through. Also, you can cut out each page using the trim line or use a separate piece of paper between pages. Have fun!

This book belongs to:

Let's practice with dot markers!

Let's practice with dot markers!

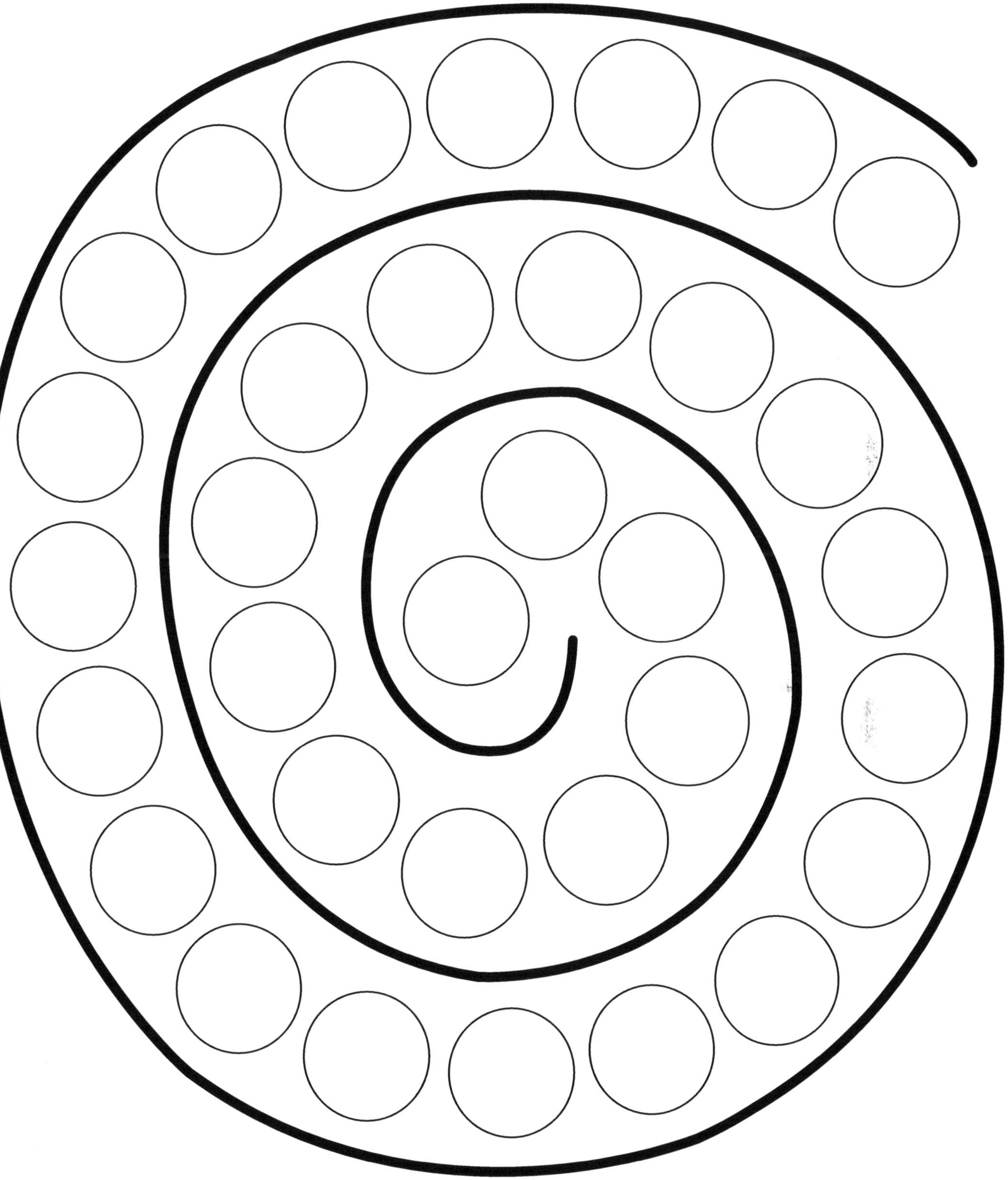

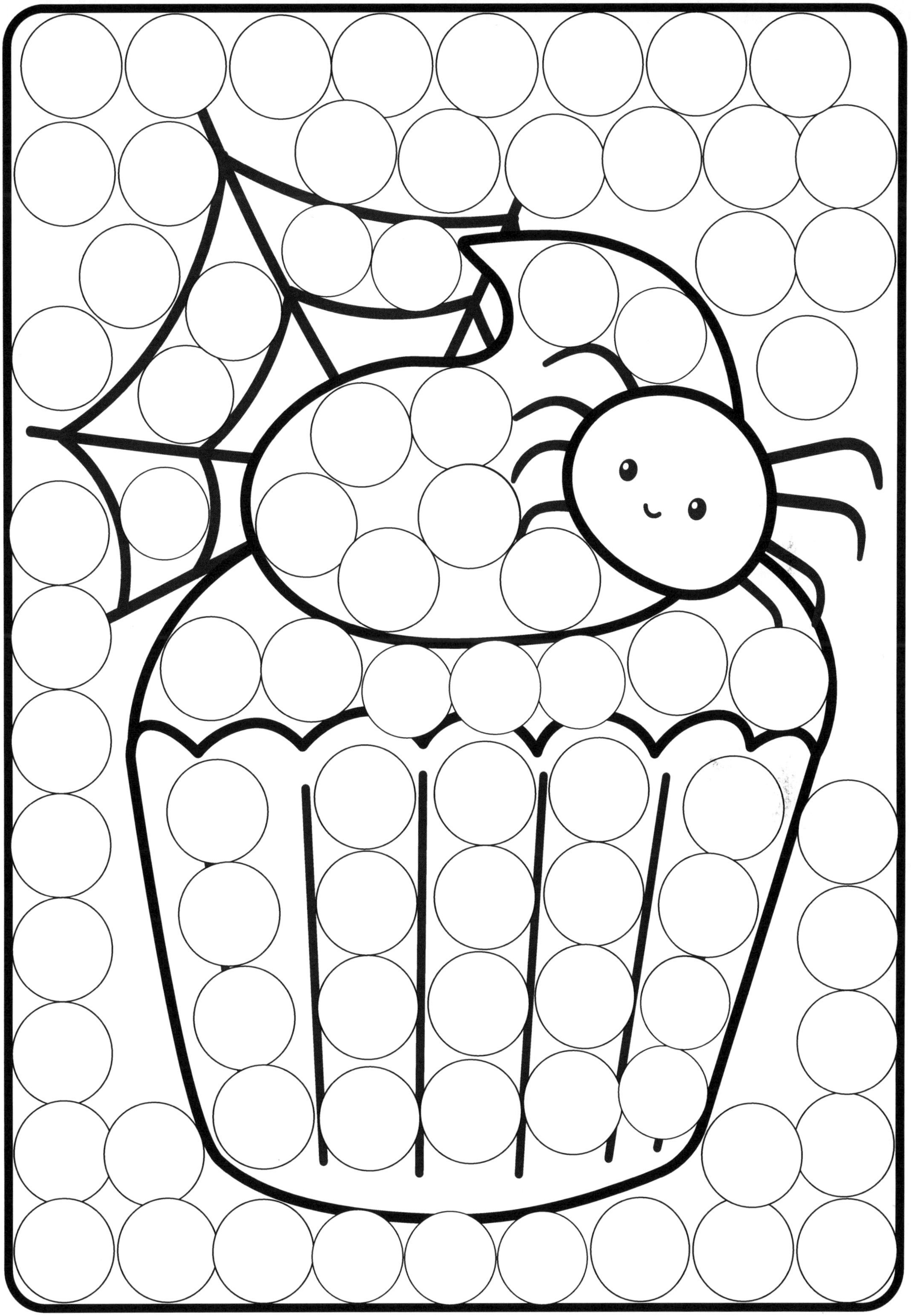

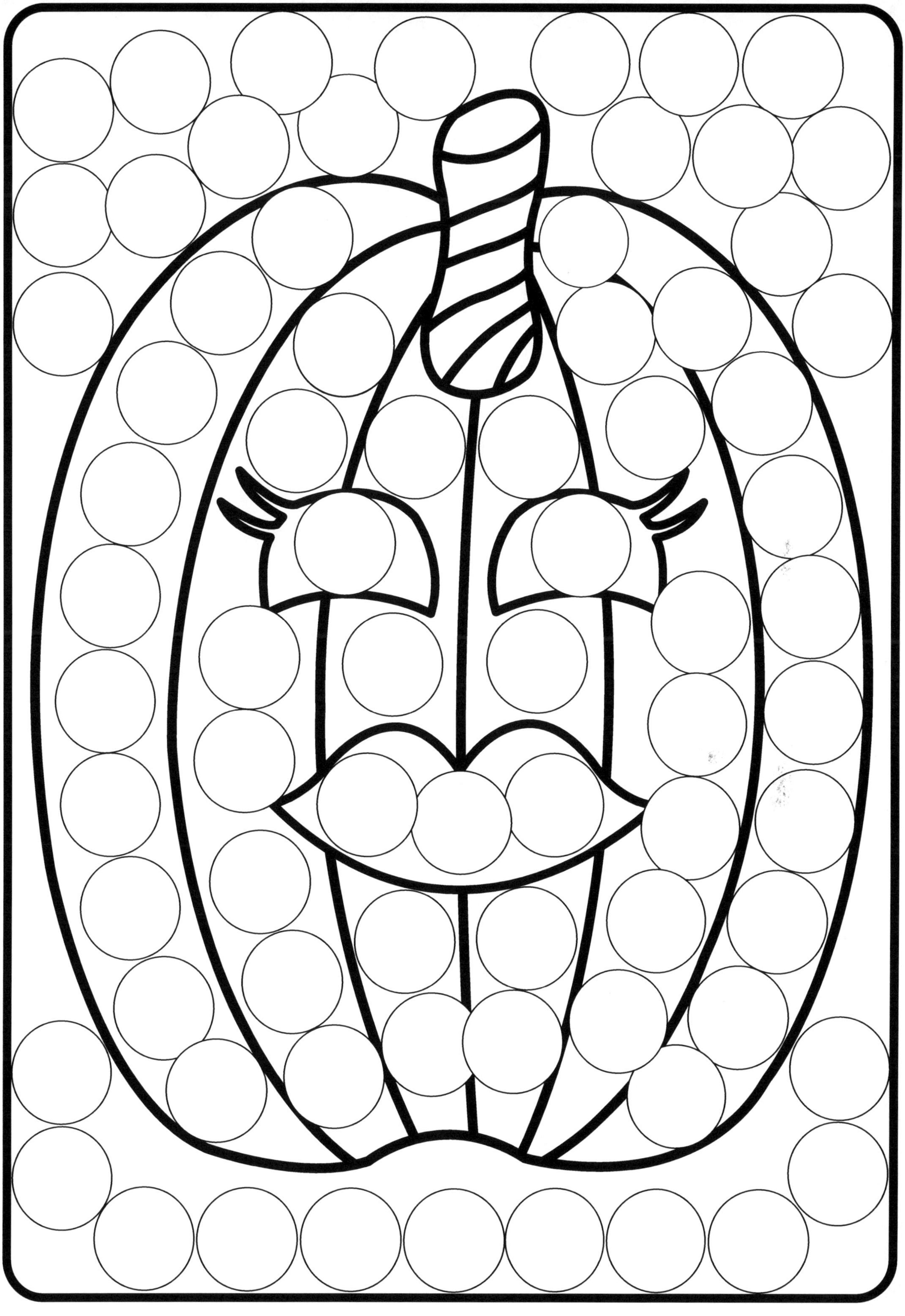

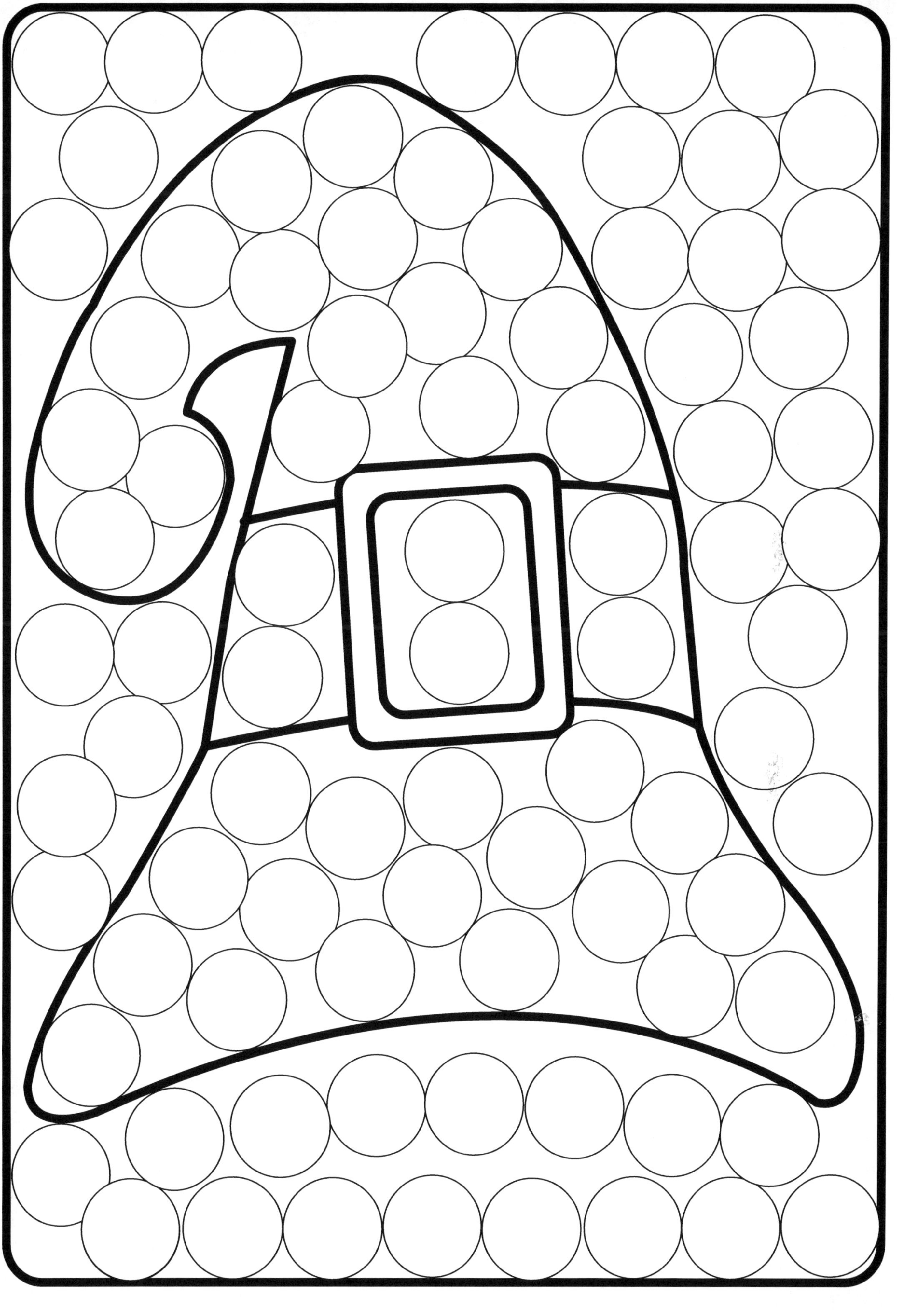

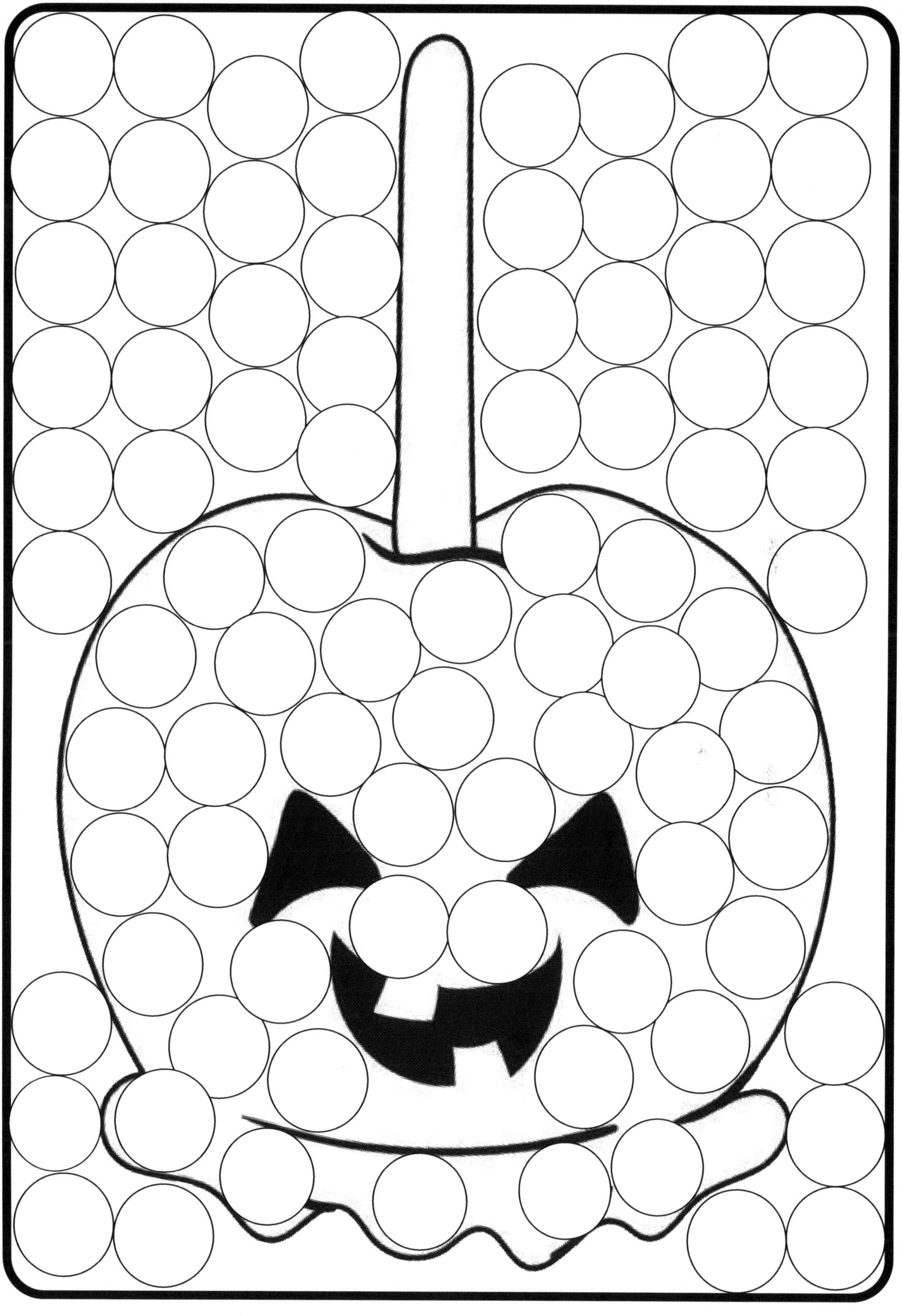